Amharic Chidlren's Book

COLORS AND SHAPES
FOR YOUR KIDS

AUTHOR
ROAN WHITE

ILLUSTRATIONS
FEDERICO BONIFACINI

©Copyright, 2018, by Roan White and Maestro Publishing Group
Illustrated by: Federico Bonifacini
All rights reserved.

No part of this book may be reproduced or transmitted in any form or by any means,
electronic or mechanical, including photocopying, recording or by any information
storage and retrieval system, without permission in writing of the copyright owner.

Printed in the United States of America

ሰማያዊ

አረንኋዴ

ብርቱካናማ

ጥቁር

ቡናማ

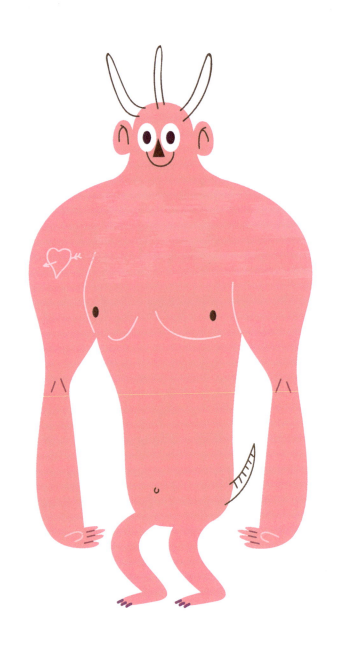

ງຣາຊ

ሶስት ማዕዘን

ከብ

አራት ማዕዘን

ጎነ እኩል ጎነ አራት

ኩልኩል ጎነ አራት

ትራፒዝየድ

ዲያመንድ ቅርጽ

ጎነ አምስት

ገነ ስድስት

ሳነ ስምንት

Made in the USA
Coppell, TX
17 November 2020